T0020162

CONTENTS

WELCOME

★ TO THE ★

SHOW!

COME ONE, COME ALL! SEE THE AMAZING CIRCUS OF FEARS!

Everyone is afraid of something. But do you have a phobia? This is a very strong fear. You may even have a phobia of something that cannot cause you any real danger.

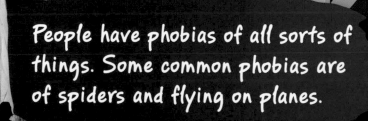

People have phobias of all sorts of things. Some common phobias are of spiders and flying on planes.

Our circus is all about real fears. Are you ready to find out what scares people the most?

Maybe you will leave the show with a brand-new phobia of your own. . . .

THE SCIENCE ★ OF ★ FEAR

Your senses are always sending information to your brain. One part of the brain that receives this information is the amygdala (uh-MIG-duh-luh).

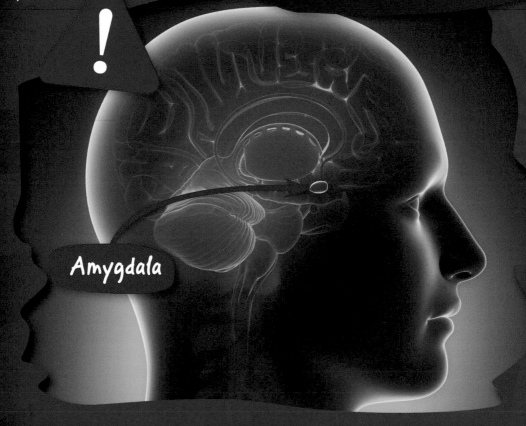

Amygdala

The amygdala quickly decides if something is scary or dangerous. It alerts your body if you hear a loud noise or see a sudden movement.

This **triggers** something called a fight-or-flight response. You might feel ready to battle or to run away. But are you really in danger?

The cortex is another part of the brain. When the amygdala raises an alarm, the cortex **evaluates** whether the danger is real. If not, it turns off the alarm. This is why we might get **startled** at first but then calm down soon after.

CREEPY SLEEP

You can't see it, and you have no power to stop it. Every night as your eyes close, you drift off into something terrifying. . . . It's sleep!

Some people actually have a phobia of sleep. For some, they may be afraid of having nightmares. They try to stay awake for as long as they can to avoid any bad dreams.

This fear can cause **anxiety** throughout the day. A person can have trouble paying attention. Then at night, they're even more worried about sleeping.

But avoiding sleep can be very unhealthy. Getting enough rest is important to help us think clearly and have enough energy throughout the day.

★ SPOOKY ★ SPACES

Imagine being in a big, empty room. If you scream, an echo will bounce off the walls and scream back. There's nothing else there!

Some people really don't like being in empty spaces. They feel better when they're surrounded by walls, mountains, or people. But when they see nothing, it makes them feel small and scared.

There are certain types of spaces that can trigger this phobia in people. They could be empty houses or wide, open fields.

Voids are endless empty places. Imagine being stuck in the middle of nowhere in outer space. Now, that's scary!

HORRIFYING ★ HEIGHTS ★

You might find the feeling of being high up exciting. Or it can be terrifying.

From the top of the stairs to the peak of a tall roller coaster, there are many scary places for people with a fear of heights. Just thinking about these high-up places makes some people's stomachs twist and turn!

Where does a fear of heights come from? Some people may have fallen from a high place when they were younger. Others may have seen someone else fall.

THE
WICKED ★ WIDE ★ WORLD

For some people, the world outside can be a scary place. They are afraid of going to unfamiliar places. Who knows what could happen out there?

People with this phobia are scared of getting into **situations** where they can't escape. They may avoid crowded places and stop themselves from taking buses or planes. These things can even cause some to have **panic** attacks.

Sometimes, this phobia starts small. A person may be worried about one place. But it can get worse, and soon the person feels afraid of everything outside their home.

A TIGHT FIT ★

Imagine being stuck in a small box with no room to move your arms and legs. The box is shut tight. There is no way out.

For some, being in small spaces feels terrifying. It makes them breathe heavily and sweat a lot. They might look everywhere they can for a way to get out.

People with a phobia of small spaces will avoid them whenever they can. They may take the stairs instead of using an elevator. Even closing a door can make a person feel trapped.

When entering a room, people who are scared of small spaces might look for any exits, such as other doors or windows. Knowing how they can get out of a room makes them feel safer.

HOME
★ (NOT SO) ★
SWEET HOME

When people think of scary places, they might imagine graveyards or dark caves. But for some people, there is someplace even worse . . . home.

People scared of going home might panic at just the thought of it. Some might even travel around the world to avoid it.

For some, this phobia began after something bad happened to them at home. Being home might remind them of this past.

Some adults fear returning to a childhood home because they feel like they failed in the outside world. People who spend a lot of time away from home, such as soldiers, might get this fear, too.

KEEP IT DOWN!

Sudden loud noises can make anybody jump. But for some people, loud noises are truly terrifying.

Maybe this is because very loud sounds can shake their whole bodies. Some are afraid because of bad things that happened after loud noises in the past.

For people with this phobia, the fear response can be set off by almost any sound. Even ordinary things, such as beeping cars, fireworks, music, or talking, can cause panic.

WORD
★ WOE ★

There once was a circus in town,
Where everyone left with a frown.
For it showed them their fears,
And left some in tears,
All without a creepy clown.

There are times words are enough,
To make people feel really rough.
Just a little rhyme,
With a bouncing **chime**,
Can fill their heads with awful stuff.

Poems can be long or short. They often come with their own rhyme and **rhythm**. No matter how they are written, poems give some people quite a scare.

The fear of poems may have started in school. Maybe a person couldn't understand the meaning behind a poem. They might have sweated and shook in their chair as the teacher looked for someone to call on.

HIDDEN
★ IN THE ★
CLOSET

Most people start the day by picking out clothes to wear. They open their closet doors to search for an outfit. Is that scary?

For some people, just the thought of clothes can frighten them. Sometimes, they're afraid of a specific piece of clothing. Other times, the fear is about any clothes.

People scared of clothes can feel like they are trapped when wearing them. Sometimes, even something small, such as a tie, can make them feel this way.

How does a fear of clothes start? It could come from being forced to wear **restrictive** clothes in the past.

★ ROTTEN ★ REFLECTION

Look into the mirror. What do you see? Most people see themselves . . . but what if you are actually looking into another world? This unlikely possiblity leaves some people shaking with fear.

If you stare into a mirror long enough, you may start to think you're seeing dark, horrible things.

Some people fear mirrors because of **superstitions**. They may believe mirrors have the power to suck in a person's soul.

Some say breaking a mirror can bring seven years of bad luck. Yikes!

Aretha Franklin was a famous musician with an incredible voice. She released many albums and performed huge shows.

Even as one of the biggest music stars in the world, Aretha had a phobia that affected her work.

In 1984, Aretha was flying on an airplane that had a lot of **turbulence**. The airplane became very shaky because of strong winds. The singer was terrified.

After that flight, Aretha never got on another plane again. Instead, she only took buses to travel to her shows.

CURTAIN
★ CLOSE ★

THANKS FOR COMING! WE HOPE YOU'VE ENJOYED EXPLORING PHOBIAS. COME BACK SOON!

Stay brave for the next time you are forced to face your fears!

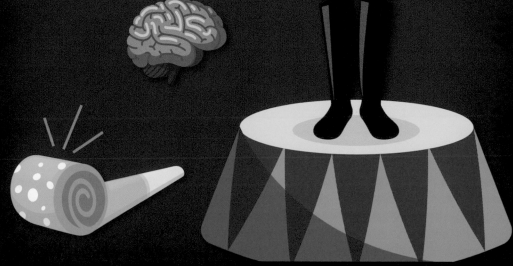

GLOSSARY

anxiety extreme nervousness or worry

chime a ringing sound

evaluates uses thinking to find out about something

panic to feel sudden and overpowering fear

restrictive limiting in a way that keeps someone from moving freely

rhythm a pattern of sounds that repeats

situations the combination of circumstances and events at a certain time

startled frightened or surprised

superstitions beliefs based on the fear of the unknown

trigger to cause someone to react

turbulence unsteady up and down movement in the air

INDEX

Read More

Colich, Abby. *Your Brain When You're Scared (Brainpower).* Minneapolis: Jump!, Inc., 2023.

Spalding, Maddie. *Understanding Phobias (Mental Health Guides).* San Diego, CA: BrightPoint Press, 2022.

Learn More Online

1. Go to **www.factsurfer.com** or scan the QR code below.

2. Enter **"World Phobias"** into the search box.

3. Click on the cover of this book to see a list of websites.